Paper
Planes

Phil Joho

Paper
Planes

Phil Joho

Published 2003 by Mud Puddle Books, Inc., 54 W. 21st St., Suite 601, New York, NY 10010, USA
Originally Published 2001, Hinkler Books Pty Ltd., 17-23 Redwood Drive, Dingley, Victoria, 3172, Australia
Copyright © 2001 by Redwood Publishing Group. All rights reserved.
Without limiting the rights under copyright above, no part of this publication may be reproduced, stored in or introduced into a retrieval system, or transmitted in any form or by any means (electronic, mechanical, photocopying, recording, or otherwise), without prior written permission of Hinkler Books Pty Ltd.
ISBN: 1-59412-021-8 • Made in China.

MUD PUDDLE BOOKS, INC.
New York, New York

Contents

Where Did Planes Come From?

There is no record of when the first paper planes were made. But people have been fascinated with the concept of flying since the time of ancient Egypt, when paper was first developed from the aquatic plant, papyrus. More than 2000 years ago the Chinese were using paper to make kites, and we know that around 300 BC the ancient Greeks were making drawings to try to understand the way birds fly. It is likely that they also made paper models of birds and flying machines, but unfortunately none have survived to the present day...

About 500 years ago Leonardo da Vinci developed and sketched a flying machine based on the movement of the wings of a bird. Maybe he made some paper models too!

We know that paper models were used to test flight theory in the early 1900s; they may have even inspired the Wright brothers in America who, in 1903, were the first people ever to fly a plane.

During World War II, the materials used to make toys were in short supply. Most of the metal produced at this time went into making tanks, guns and bullets. Children played with toys made from wood and paper and in the 1940s and 50s building and flying paper planes became very popular.

Some people say that the top-secret B-2 stealth bomber was developed with the aid of paper models. When you are familiar with the construction techniques you can develop your own designs - perhaps for the space travel of the future!

4

Why Do Planes Fly?

If you let go of a piece of flat paper it will turn and flap before landing on the floor. If you repeat this action several times, the paper will seldom fall in the same way or land in the same place - this is unstable movement, and can't really be called *flight*.

For a piece of paper to *really* fly it should stay in the air for a reasonable length of time and travel in a predictable way. When you change the paper's shape to make it more streamlined, maybe by shaping it into a simple dart, it will fall smoothly to the floor and land in the same general place. This flight is more predictable. To enable the dart or plane to stay in the air longer and achieve real flight, we need to create what is known as *lift* to counter the *weight* of the paper.

The same principles apply to both powered and unpowered flight. Aeroplanes are an example of powered flight - the engine is provided for extra lift to counteract the heavy weight of the aircraft. Gliders are made of very lightweight materials so they can fly without power, though they first need to be towed into the air. Paper planes are gliders too - and they only need a human arm to launch them!

To achieve lift an aircraft's wings are angled so that the front edges are higher than the back edges, and this makes the air speed up as it goes over the curved top of the wings. The air going under the wing slows down because it meets the back of the wing that has been tilted down. The difference in the speed that the air travels above and below the wing is what creates the lift. You can test this theory by holding a strip of paper with the short end to your mouth, and blowing across the top of it. The paper will 'lift' as you blow.

Drag and thrust also influence the aircraft's flight. The thrust of your throw propels your plane forward, but once it has been launched, air resistance creates drag, pushing against the plane's forward motion. Once you have made your plane, you can experiment with its flying patterns by making tiny adjustments to its wing and tail shapes.

There is much more to read and learn about flight, but let's make our own paper planes and see what happens as we fly them ...

Lift

Drag

Weight

Thrust

Some Tips to Help Your Planes Fly at Their Best

These flying tips will help you achieve great things with your planes.

Use standard sized paper (often referred to as A4) which is about 297mm x 210mm (or 11.7" x 8.3") unless otherwise instructed (one of our models begins as a square shape).

Make sure that you fold carefully, running your finger over each fold to make sure it is crisp. Use a hard surface like a table or bench top - not carpet, for instance.

If, during the making of your plane, the instructions suddenly don't seem to make sense, try undoing the last few folds and checking the diagrams and instructions again. You might have missed a tiny detail that will make all the difference.

Different designs of plane respond to different ways of being launched. As you launch your plane, try using your elbow instead of flicking your wrist. Some designs respond better to a 'push' or gentle 'thrust' in to the air rather than a hard throw.

If your plane dives sharply towards the ground, slightly bend *up* the back edges of the wings. This will help the nose point more upwards in flight and give the plane more *lift*.

If, on the other hand, your plane flies sharply upwards then falls backward towards the ground, adjust the back edges of the wings *down* to straighten the flight path.

Remember to always fly safely - never point or launch your plane *at* anybody. Always fly your plane well clear of overhead wires and never near any roads.

Construction Terms

We have included a list of the basic building terms used to help you understand the step-by-step instructions for each model.

Single headed arrow:
means that you *fold* the paper as shown and *leave it folded*

Double headed arrow:
means that you *fold* the paper as shown and then open it out again so the paper is flat, but now it has a *crease* in it

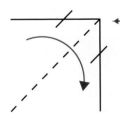

Pairs of marked lines:
lines marked with one or two dashes mean that when the appropriate fold is made the mark(s) on each line will meet exactly

Valley fold:
an *evenly dotted line* indicates that the paper should be folded to make a valley, with the fold being *lower* than the surrounding paper

Mountain fold:
an *unevenly dotted line* (a combination of dots and dashes) tells you to make the fold so that it is *higher* than the surrounding paper

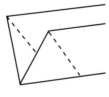

Inward push-back fold:
is a diagonal crease made across the corner of an *already-folded* piece of paper, which is then pushed back inside the fold

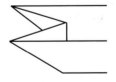

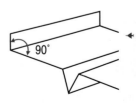

90 degree angle:
also referred as 90° and a *right angle*

7

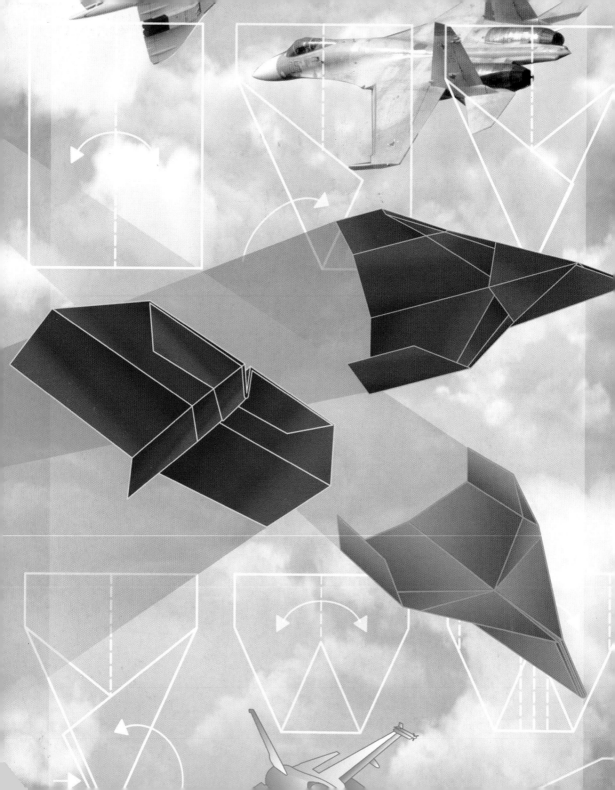

For the Beginner

The Classic

This well-known and loved design is a great one to start on. It's easy to achieve a good result, and as long as you take time to fold with care, it will fly really well.

Don't throw this one too hard - a gentle to medium strength launch is fine.

1

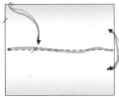

1. Fold sheet of paper in half and then open again (to make a crease). Then fold corner to look like Figure 2.

4

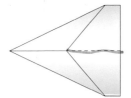

4. Then fold corners over again, so they meet in the middle...

2

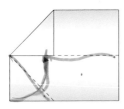

2. Repeat with other corner.

5

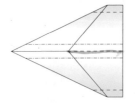

5. ...to look like this.

3

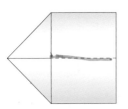

3. Your plane should look like this.

6

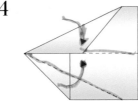

6. Now to make the wings and flaps. Make the fuselage or body about 25mm (1") deep and the flaps about 20mm (0.75") high. Make sure these folds are bent at right angles (90º).

The Snub Nose

This is another traditional or classic design that flies well with a minimum strength throw.

1

1.
Fold sheet of paper in half and then open again (to make a crease).

2

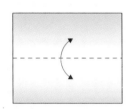

2.
Fold corner over as shown, keeping bottom point at the centre fold.

5

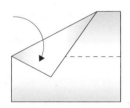

5.
Turn plane over to other side, and fold tip over...

3

fold flap under

3.
Fold other side, then fold the overlapping flap under. Make sure that points A & B on your plane are the same as the diagram.

6

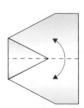

6.
...to look like this. Then fold down the middle.

4

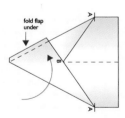

4.
This is how your plane should look after the flap is folded under.

7

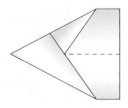

7.
Last thing to do is fold the wings and flaps. Again, around 25mm (1") for the wings and 20mm (0.75") for the flaps.

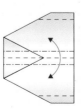

11

The Speed Demon

If your folding is crisp and carefully done you'll soon see why this plane is called the Speed Demon!
Make a few with friends and see whose will fly furthest.

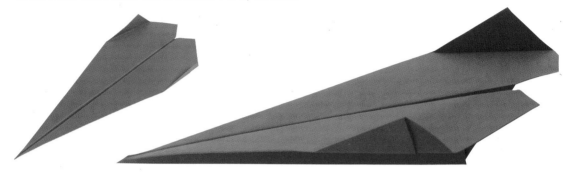

1

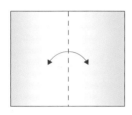

1. Fold sheet of paper in half and then open again (crease).

4

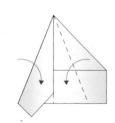

4. Then fold these corners over again. Make sure they meet in the middle.

2

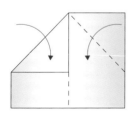

2. Fold corner in as shown, repeat with the other corner ...

5

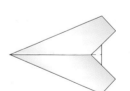

5. Your plane should now look like this.

3

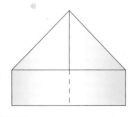

3. ... to look like this.

6

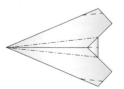

6. Make the wings and flaps according to the diagram. The narrower the wings are - the faster your plane will fly!

The Floater

This plane really floats - another word for gliding. This is also a good one to share with friends. The wider wingspan means it won't fly as fast as the Demon but it will stay in the air longer and land gracefully.

1

1. Once again, fold your sheet of paper in half and open again (crease).

2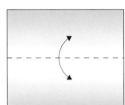

2. Fold corner over as shown, then repeat with the other corner ...

3

3. ... to look like this. Now fold the point over ...

4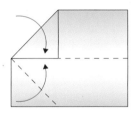

4. ... so that it looks like this. The next step is to fold in the corner.

5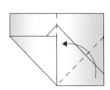

5. Repeat with other side.

6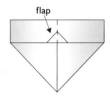

flap

6. Your plane should be like this diagram, with a small flap sticking out.

7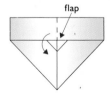

flap

7. Fold this flap over. Note that this is a view of the bottom of the plane.

8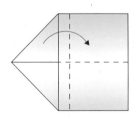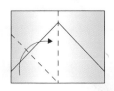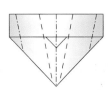

8. Fold the plane down the middle, fold the wings, then the flaps at right angles and turn the model over to fly it.

13

B-52 Bomber

This is a slow-flying, long-range plane. It may need some slight wing adjustments for optimum flying. Test it first with different launching techniques and then adjust gently.

1

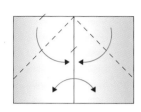

1. Fold in half to crease, then fold corners in.

2

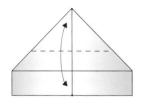

2. Fold the point down to the lower edge, then open out to make a crease.

3

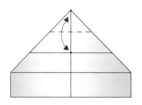

3. Fold the point over to the crease made in Step 2. Leave folded.

4

4. Then fold so the point meets the crease made in Step 2.

5

5. Fold the edge again so that the crease made in Step 2 now turns into a fold!

6

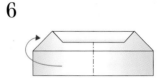

6. This is how the plane now looks. Note this is a bottom view.

7

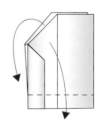

7. Fold point over to the crease made in Step 2.

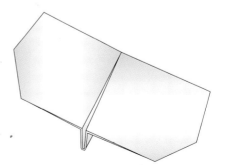

The Wing-Tipped Square

This is an easy plane to make, but it will fly all the better for a bit of 'tweaking'. If the plane dives you need to bend the wings up slightly. If it climbs before diving, you need to bend the wings slightly downwards. If it veers right or left, bend the rudder - the central lower part - to the opposite side.

1

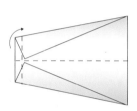

1. Taking the usual sized paper, make a vertical crease down the centre, then make valley folds along the diagonal lines at each side. The corners should meet at the centre crease.

2

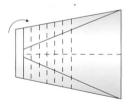

2. Make a valley fold up from the bottom of the plane, as shown. Ensure the paper is well creased.

3

3. Fold over three more times, about 25mm (1") for each fold.

4

4. Make 3 more folds again tucking any excess bulges into the folds as you go.

5

5. Make a mountain fold along the plane's centreline.

6

6. Fold the wings and flaps as shown.

7

7. Make sure your flaps are neat right angles and angle the wings so that the outer edges lie above the plane body, forming a slight "Y" shape when you look at it from the front.

17

For the More Advanced

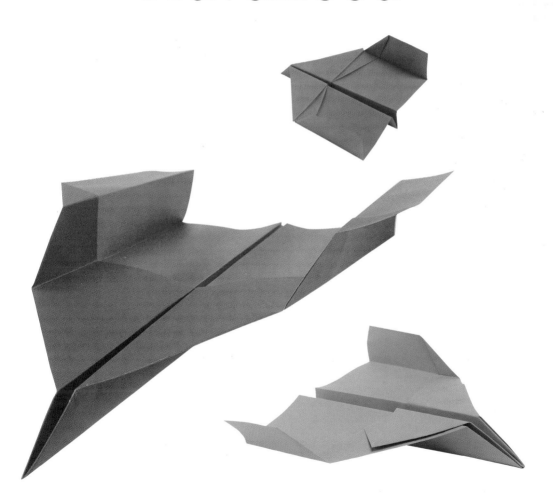

19

The Eagle

If you've ever watched a soaring eagle, you'll know that it uses its huge wingspan to cruise on the warm air currents high in the sky. See if you can get this plane to stay in the air for longer than usual.

1

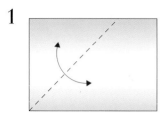

1. Make a diagonal valley fold, then unfold to leave a crease.

6

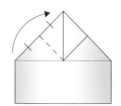

6. Repeat with the other side.

2

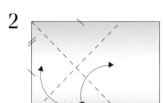

2. Repeat with the other edge.

7a

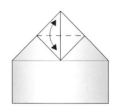

7. Fold the whole of the point at the front down to the edge of the paper.

3

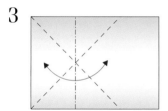

3. Make a mountain fold in the middle to add another crease.

7b

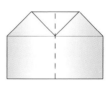

4

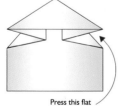

Press this flat

4. Push the sides in and fold down. If you made sharp creases in the previous steps, this will be easy.

8

8. Fold in half and make the wings. The fuselage should be about 25mm (1") deep.

5

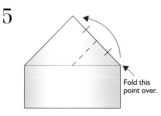

Fold this point over.

5. Fold the point of the upper triangular layer over, so it meets the top.

21

Ye Old Faithful

This plane has been around for many years and is still an all-time favourite.

Its design allows it to fly very straight and it is easy to vary the amount of lift. It can also handle most wind conditions.

We're moving into some harder-to-create designs now, so persevere if you don't get your plane to fly perfectly first time.

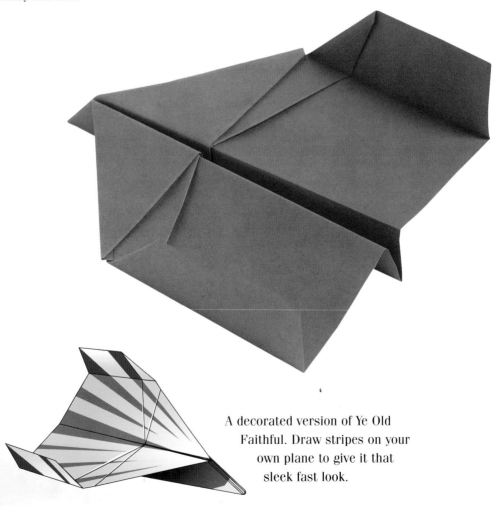

A decorated version of Ye Old Faithful. Draw stripes on your own plane to give it that sleek fast look.

22

1

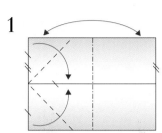

1. Using the standard beginning, make the illustrated folds.

4

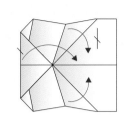

4. This stage looks a bit strange, but if your previous creases are sharp, it should be easy to make the model look like the next diagram.

2

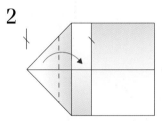

2. This model is intended to fly flat. If you want to get more lift, move the vertical fold so the point of the paper is further to the left.

5

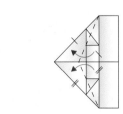

5. This stage looks worse than it is. You need to fold the flaps under the large triangle at the left of the diagram. It is easier if you almost unfold the other half of the plane to make each fold.

3

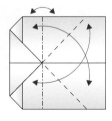

3. Make sure that you just crease the paper here, the diagonal creases should intersect with the horizontal centre line and the vertical crease. That is, don't fold over so that the edges meet.

6

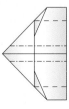

6. Now to the final stage. As a rough guide, make the fuselage or body of the plane about 2cm (0.75") deep, and the vertical flaps about 3cm (1.25") deep. Note that as these last two folds have a large influence on how the plane will fly, they need to be as parallel as possible to the sides of the paper, and the flaps should be folded at 90°.

23

The Spy

This plane has been around almost as long as Ye Old Faithful, and with practice, can also be made into a superb flier.

The amount of lift can be varied to make a flat flier or a gentle glider. This plane may actually fly better when launched with less speed. Go ahead and experiment!

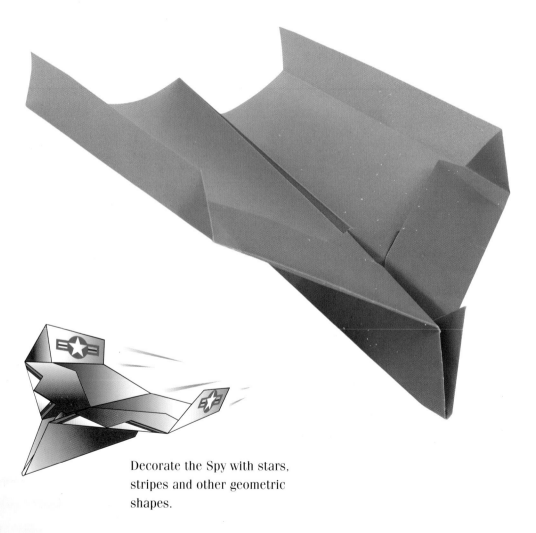

Decorate the Spy with stars, stripes and other geometric shapes.

24

1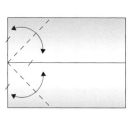

1. The standard beginning - crease along the middle horizontal to start with, then crease the corners.

2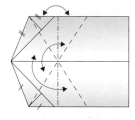

2. Now fold over the corners.

3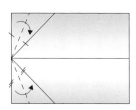

3. This section looks worse than it is. Follow the guidelines and make nice sharp creases. Use the single line dashes as your guide for folding, and the double-line dashes on the other side.

4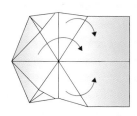

4. Fold in to make the next picture. This is a technique you need to get used to.

5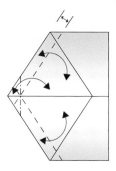

5. This is sometimes called the 'flight' fold; it determines how much lift the plane has. First make a vertical mountain crease as shown, then valley creases parallel with the diagonal front edges.

As a guide, the distance (shown in the diagram) needs to be somewhere between 25mm and 35mm (1" and 1.5"). When experimenting, I found a fold at 30mm (1.25") produced a plane that glides nicely. Note that the smaller this measurement is, the more lift the plane will have.

Fold the diagonal creases down at the same time so that the 'nose' sits straight up in a small triangular shape at the centre. Next place the tip of a pencil inside the triangular flap to open it out. Flatten the flap into a diamond shape so that it looks like diagram 6.

6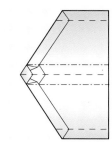

6. The last step is to make the wings and the flaps. Fold the plane down the centre in a valley fold. Make mountain folds about 25mm (1") from the centre line, and the flaps should take up about a third of the remaining wing - also 25mm (1"). Fold the flaps at right angles to the wings.

25

The Spear

This plane is great for throwing flat and hard - but it is by no means just a dart. The Spear is very easy to fly and won't need constant adjustment. You can pick it straight up off the floor and throw it again. Have fun!

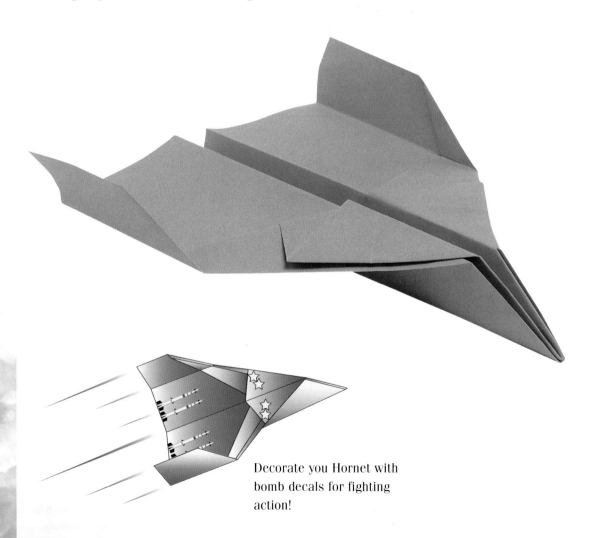

Decorate you Hornet with bomb decals for fighting action!

26

1

1. Using the usual sized paper, crease the horizontal fold, then make the diagonal folds as shown, and open out again.

4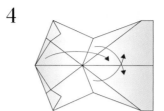

4. As with previous models, if the creases are sharp then this step should be relatively easy. The two flaps that go on the inside will have to lie on top of each other as they both cross over the horizontal fold line.

2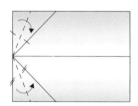

2. Fold again so the edge of the paper and the crease from the previous fold meet.

5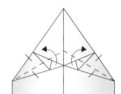

5. This fold is a bit tricky. The two flaps, which are on the inside, need to be folded under the upper layer. It is easier if you unfold the other side to give you room to make the fold for each side.

3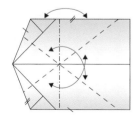

3. Make the two diagonal creases and then one vertical crease to intersect the diagonal ones. Note that the vertical one is a mountain crease.

6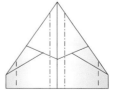

6. Again, as a rough guide make the fuselage or body of the plane about 20mm (0.75") deep, and the vertical flaps about 30mm (1.25") deep. Make sure that these folds are parallel.

The Brick

This plane is a relatively new design and has quite a slow flight - so it has became known as a 'brick'.

However, despite this affectionate nickname, this model flies in a wonderful trajectory. It can be either reasonably slow or quite fast, which is unusual for paper planes.

Slow launching may increase flight time, depending on how well you have folded the plane. It's up to you to experiment.

28

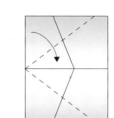

1

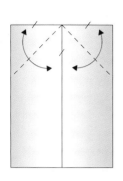

1. Using the standard size paper, make the usual crease down the middle and two creases at the left-hand corners.

2

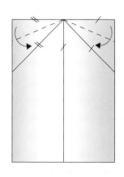

2. Then fold the corners again as shown, ensuring that the creases are made so that the marked edges join up well.

3

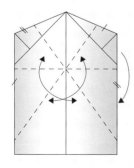

3. This is the same fold as several of the previous planes - except note that the vertical crease is a valley fold, not a mountain this time. Make a valley fold along the vertical crease.

4

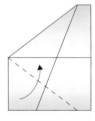

4. Fold down the top left corner along the valley crease.

5

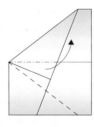

5. Fold up bottom left corner along its valley crease.

6a

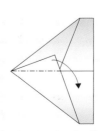

6b

6. In the top flap, make a mountain fold along the plane's centre line. Repeat with the other top flap so that both flaps meet neatly along the centre line.

29

7

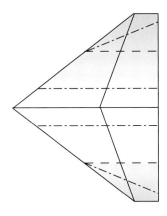

7. Last but not least is the all-important step of folding the wings - this time make the fuselage or body around 20mm (0.75") deep. The flaps should then take up about half the remaining wing width. With this plane you need to then make another fold to make the upright flaps by folding over the edges - make sure that these folds are at right-angles.

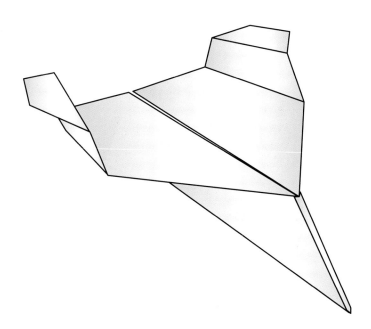

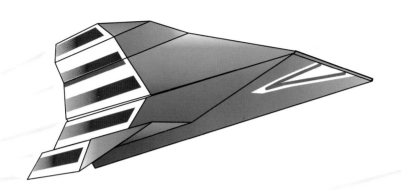

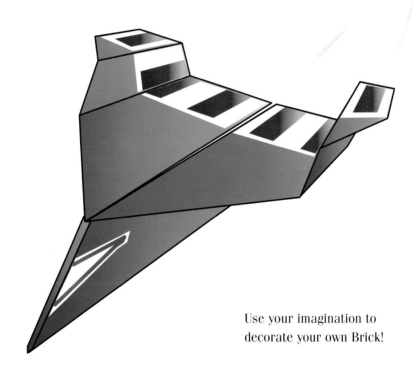

Use your imagination to
decorate your own Brick!

31

The Seaplane

Of course, paper planes and water are not a good combination, but this plane is designed along the lines of the seaplanes that land on water to unload their passengers at exotic beachside locations. This is an interesting plane to fly. It has a tendency to be unstable, so extra strong paper is recommended.

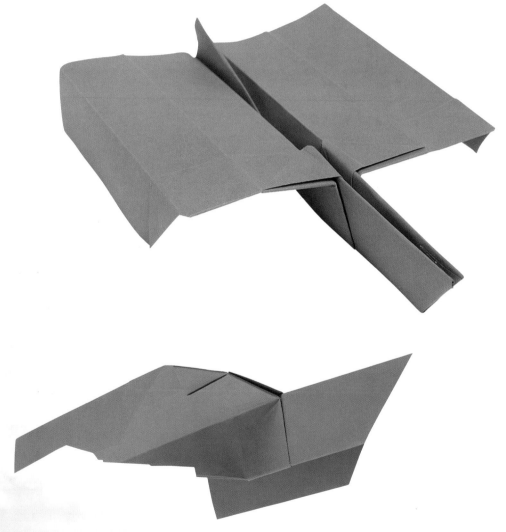

1

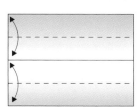

1. Using strong paper, make a horizontal crease down the centre. Make two valley creases either side by folding the upper and lower edges to the centre crease.

4

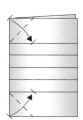

4. Make two diagonal valley folds.

2

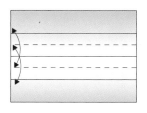

2. Make two more valley creases either side of the centre line.

5

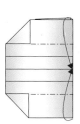

5. Remake mountain folds on the upper layer only. This means that part of the previous steps' folds will tuck under the upper layer.

3

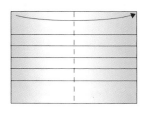

3. Now make a vertical valley fold.

6

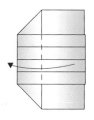

6. Make a vertical valley fold as shown.

7

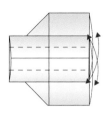

7. Make two valley folds. These will be a continuation of the folds already made in the lower layer.

10

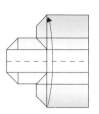

10. Fold plane in half along centre line.

8

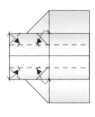

8. Make two inward push-back folds as shown in the upper layer, and two valley folds in the outer corners.
To make the inward push-back fold, make diagonal creases first, then open out and push the outer edge inside and fold over again.

11

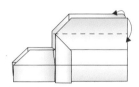

11. Make two valley folds, one each side.

9

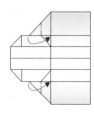

9. In the lower layer, make a mountain fold.

12

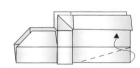

12. Make another inward push-back fold as shown.

34

13

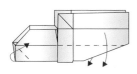

13. To make the wings, make two valley folds, one each side. Then make an inward push-back fold for the nose of the plane.

14

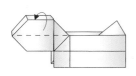

14. Remake the mountain fold on the near side of the plane's nose. Tuck it in and fold over the centre piece to 'lock' in place.

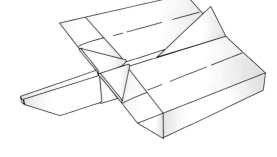

15

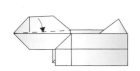

15. Remake the valley fold on the other side, tuck in and you've finished.

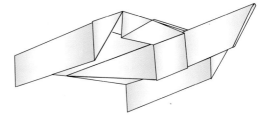

Compare your plane with the views below to see you have it right.

A Tip:

if you have trouble with this amount of folding the first time around, use a lightweight sheet of paper first and take it slowly until you feel you have the folding techniques correct. Then try the sheet of strong paper. But remember, this plane will fly better when you use heavier paper.

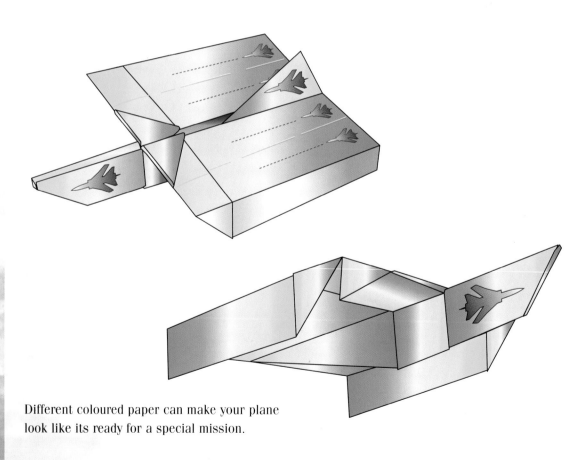

Different coloured paper can make your plane look like its ready for a special mission.

Paper Concorde

This design is based on the previous Seaplane model, but has a more streamlined nose. You'll need strong paper for its construction, and a strong thrust to launch it. It's worth the effort.

The first seven step of the Paper Concord are just
like the Seaplane so you are already half way there...

5

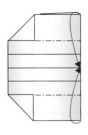

1. Using strong
paper, make a
horizontal crease
down the centre.
Make two valley
creases either side
by folding the upper
and lower edges to
the centre crease.

5. Remake
mountain
folds on the upper
layer only. This
means that part of
the previous steps'
folds will tuck under
the upper layer.

1

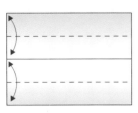

6

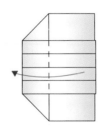

2. Make two
more valley
creases either side of
the centre line.

6. Make a
vertical
valley fold as
shown.

2

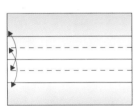

7

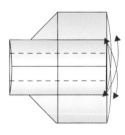

3. Now make a
vertical valley
fold.

7. Make two
valley folds.
These will be a
continuation of the
folds already made
in the lower layer.

3

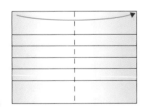

4

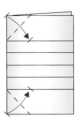

8

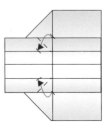

4. Make two
diagonal
valley folds.

8. Make two
inward
push-back folds
where shown.

9

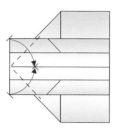

9. Fold the corners down to meet at the centre line.

13

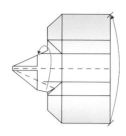

13. Now fold your plane down the centre in a valley fold. Take the other half of the plane's nose and make a valley fold, folding it over and tucking the edge down into the pocket to 'lock' it together.

10

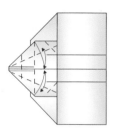

10. Make two valley folds and open out again.

14

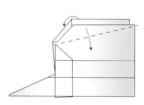

14. Now for the wings. Make a valley fold in each one where indicated.

11

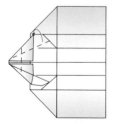

11. Using the crease made in the last step, make one inward push-back fold. Don't make the other yet.

15

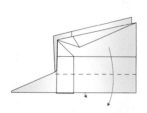

15. Make a valley fold on each side of the body of the plane to give it its distinctive shape.

12

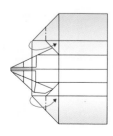

12. Make a mountain fold on the lower layer of your plane as shown.

Does your plane look like this?

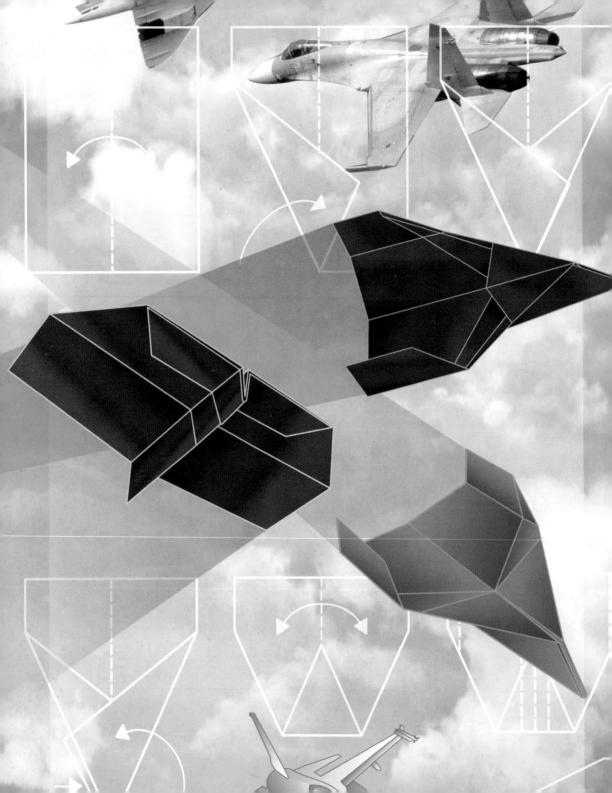

For the Experts

The Dog Fighter

This streamlined design is a little tricky to fold, but looks great and flies beautifully.
Try making several with your friends and launching them all at once for a real dogfight!

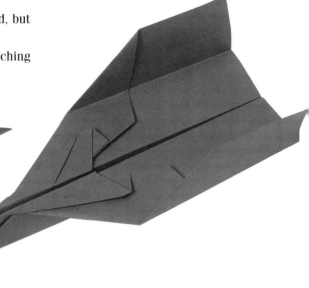

1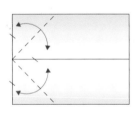

1. Using ordinary weight paper, make a horizontal crease and two diagonal creases.

3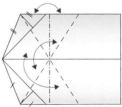

3. As we have done before, make the two diagonal valley creases and the vertical mountain crease as shown.

2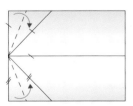

2. Create valley folds by folding the top edges down to meet the creases made in the last step.

4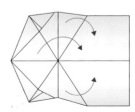

4. If creases made in Step 3 were crisp and accurate, this fold should be easy. Fold the sides into the middle, and flatten the diamond shape down firmly.

5

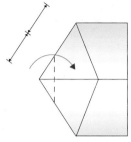

5. This is a new instruction - consider yourself an expert when it's complete.

As illustrated, make a firm valley crease then open out again. Now lift the top flap (and only the top flap) of the diamond and fold it back along the crease just made. Flatten the two sides down so that they almost meet in the centre. It seems an unnatural fold to begin with, but it's a useful plane-making technique.

6

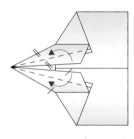

6. For this stage you need to fold the top flaps away from the centre, as shown.

7

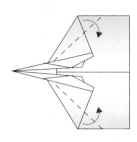

7. We are nearly there! Fold the side flaps in, as far as you can without disturbing the top half of the plane. Make them so that the edges meet close in under the folds that you made in the previous step.

8

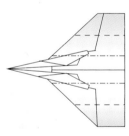

8. Now to make the wings. I suggest around 25mm (1") for the fuselage and 37mm (about 1.5") for the flaps. Make all the folds to 90°, and ensure that the surfaces are flat.

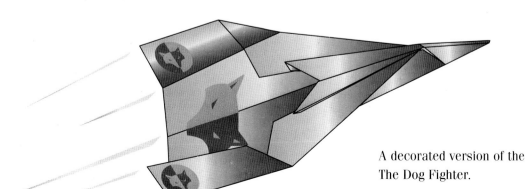

A decorated version of the The Dog Fighter.

The Hornet

This plane is an old, and unfortunately a temperamental, classic. Sometimes, even if you take the utmost care when constructing this plane, the result can be unpredictable.

Occasionally they fly badly, rolling over continuously during flight. But it's worth making because, when you get it right, the plane is a beauty - it will fly a very long distance.

It has almost no lift, making it a real speed merchant - it could turn into a lethal weapon, so make sure you never point your plane at anybody. With a bit of persistence to get it flying right, this plane will become No.1 in your squadron.

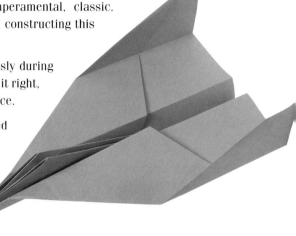

1

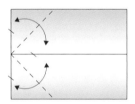

1. Make a horizontal crease along the centre and two valley creases at the left-hand corners.

3

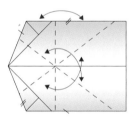

3. Now make diagonal valley folds where marked and a vertical mountain crease to intersect them.

2

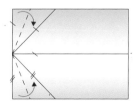

2. Make another diagonal valley fold by folding the top edges to line up with the crease made in step 1.

4

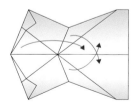

4. If the previous steps' folds are crisp and even, this step should be easy to perform. Gently fold the sides (mountain fold) in to the centre and bring the left side of the paper (the front of the plane) to fold over flat as shown in the next diagram. The sides should overlap under the top flap.

5

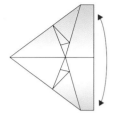

5. To make the next fold easier, fold the entire plane in half in a mountain fold then open out.

6a

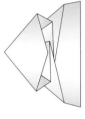

6b

6. This step is a little tricky. You need to almost unfold a couple of the previous steps so that the two folds that overlap under the flap fold back onto their own sides. The creases that make this possible should already be there from Step 5. The diagrams show how the folds should be made.

7

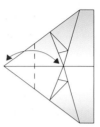

7. Here we use the same technique that we learned for the Dog Fighter. Make a vertical valley crease as shown, so that the point on the left lines up with the opposite point of the 'arrowhead' shape in the top layer of the model. Remake the fold by lifting the right side of the flap over towards the point. Make sure you only lift the upper layer. There will be some resistance to this fold. Now flatten the sides so that they meet along the centre.

8

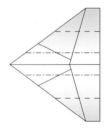

8. Finally, all the hard work is done. We just need to fold the wings and flaps. Make the fuselage around 20mm (0.75") deep. The mountain folds should only be in the lower layer. Leave the centre to stick up to make the Hornet's cockpit. Make the flaps around half the remaining wing width, and as usual, the folds should be at 90°.

A decorated version of The Hornet.

Space Flight

The challenge here is not to see how far or how fast this model can fly, but how long it will stay in the air! When it is perfectly balanced the simple lines of this model allow it to glide and float - the challenge for you is to get it that way.

This time you need a square piece of paper - rather than the usual oblong shape.

1

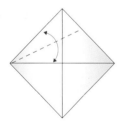

1. Beginning with a square piece of paper creased in half along both diagonals, fold one edge to the horizontal centre then unfold.

3

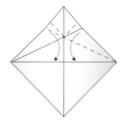

3. Fold both sides in at the same time, so that a small triangle is formed in the middle. Flatten the triangle to the right.

2

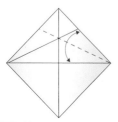

2. Repeat this crease on the other side.

4

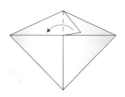

4. Now fold the triangle to the left to ensure the crease is sharp.

5

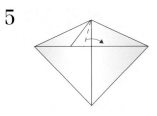

5. Lift the triangle in the centre and flatten it so both sides are equal and the vertical creases line up.

You could use a pencil to help open out this flap.

6

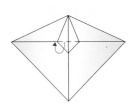

6. Next tuck the triangular flap under the layers which have been formed.

7

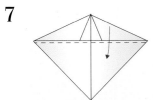

7. Fold down the top section using your first halfway crease as a guide.

8

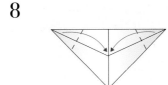

8. Fold each sharp corner into the shallow inner corner as shown.

9

9. Now unfold both corners.

10

10. Use the existing creases to allow the wings to curve a little. See the profile diagram.

Some tips:

If the wings are at different angles, this plane will fly in a loop. Launch it from as high as you can - stand tall and hold it by the tail with your arm straight up in the air - gently launch it without effort. Finally, try launching this model upside down - it will right itself while it flies.

Index

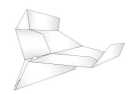

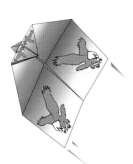

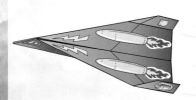